The Fabian Society

The Fabian Society is Britain's leading left of centre think tank and political society, committed to creating the political ideas and policy debates which can shape the future of progressive politics.

With over 300 Fabian MPs, MEPs, Peers, MSPs and AMs, the Society plays an unparalleled role in linking the ability to influence policy debates at the highest level with vigorous grassroots debate among our growing membership of over 7000 people, 70 local branches meeting regularly throughout Britain and a vibrant Young Fabian section organising its own activities. Fabian publications, events and ideas therefore reach and influence a wider audience than those of any comparable think tank. The Society is unique among think tanks in being a thriving, democratically-constituted membership organisation, affiliated to the Labour Party but organisationally and editorially independent.

For over 120 years Fabians have been central to every important renewal and revision of left of centre thinking. The Fabian commitment to open and participatory debate is as important today as ever before as we explore the ideas, politics and policies which will define the next generation of progressive politics in Britain, Europe and around the world. Find out more at **www.fabians.org.uk**

Fabian Society
11 Dartmouth Street
London SW1H 9BN
www.fabians.org.uk

Fabian ideas
Editorial Director: Tom Hampson

First published 2007

ISBN 978-0-7163-0622-1
ISSN 1746-1146

British Library Cataloguing in Publication data.
A catalogue record for this book is available from the British Library.

Printed and bound by Bell & Bain, Glasgow

Facing Out
How party politics must change to build a progressive society

by Tim Horton, David Pinto-Duschinsky
and Jessica Studdert

About the authors

Tim Horton is the Research Director of the Fabian Society. He is a member of Walthamstow CLP and branch secretary of Walthamstow West Labour Party.

David Pinto-Duschinsky is a Research Associate at the Fabian Society. He worked previously as a special advisor at the Home Office and at the Prime Minister's Strategy Unit. He is a member of Hackney North and Stoke Newington CLP.

Jessica Studdert is a Researcher and the Events Director at the Fabian Society. She has been a social policy research analyst at the Citizen's Advice Bureau. She is a member of Islington South CLP.

Acknowledgments

The authors are grateful to Sunder Katwala, Rachael Jolley, Hannah Jameson, Leigh Marshall, Shazia Chaudhry, Lorriann Robinson and Tom Hampson at the Fabian Society for the research support they provided to the project. The authors also benefited from talking to many people who contributed their time and expertise to the project. We would like to thank in particular Nick Anstead, Luke Bruce, Tony Burton, Joe Caluori, Anne Campbell, Nita Clarke, David Coats, Ben Coffman, Stella Creasy, John Cryer, John Denham, Katie Elliott, Justin Fisher, John Healey, Ian Gibson, Brian Keegan, John Lloyd, Adrian Lovett, Fiona MacTaggart, Seema Malhotra, Kirsty McNeill, Jon Pearce, Paul Richards, Greg Rosen, Meg Russell, Martin Salter, Anne Sassoon, Jonathan Smith, Gerry Stoker, David Sullivan, Emily Thornberry, Paul Webb and Daniel Zeichner. However, the views expressed in the pamphlet are those of the authors alone and the input of any individual does not imply endorsement of the views or recommendations outlined here.

Contents

Introduction

Reconnecting people to politics is the issue of the moment. Alongside public scrutiny of our constitutional settlement, and the rights and responsibilities of citizenship, political renewal must also involve thinking again about how parties can contribute to strengthening democracy.

We reject the idea that political parties are a relic of the past, and show how populist frustration with party politics can often demonstrate a refusal to confront the compromises and trade-offs that remain the essence of democracy. Yet parties will need to change to remain relevant, and to respond to the transformations in society that are threatening all political parties.

The Labour Party, under new leadership, has a chance to take stock of the future organisational challenges it faces. The central question must be how Labour can remain at the forefront of campaigning for, and achieving, progressive social change. We believe that this will demand major changes in how the Party thinks, organises and acts.

As a decade of power shows, Labour has become better at winning elections than at any time in its history. This matters. Parties need to hold power, nationally and locally, to make change. But they must also be more than election-winning machines. The way the Party and wider movement is currently organised puts much less emphasis than is needed on two other important goals: achieving long-term shifts in political opinion, and ensuring the participation and engagement of people to make political success sustainable.

This can only happen if we can change the culture of our party politics, and begin a different type of discussion inside the Party about reform. This will be difficult. Too often, the echoes of political battles fought, won and lost over a generation ago still dominate.

Too many, on all sides, use proposals about reform as an instrumental way to fight policy battles by proxy. And we seem to be stuck with a debate where ministers often stress the need for a rigid and disciplined 'top down' party for electoral success while disaffected members demand a 'bottom up' party for democratic legitimacy. But both, in their different ways, share a 'one size fits all' mentality – debating only who should be in charge of a monolithic party. Neither model offers an attractive or effective vision for Labour's future. We risk talking only amongst and about ourselves, rather than about how the Party can best face outwards and advocate progressive change in society.

Our vision is different. Of course, a successful party must have leadership and organisation at the centre, working effectively with genuine energy and engagement which comes from participation at all levels. But it must be a plural and open party at every level, which is comfortable with diversity of opinion and which reaches out and establishes new habits of working with others at national and local level. Our polling shows that many progressives outside the Party would get more involved with and campaign alongside Labour without joining up, but are not currently offered the right opportunities for this. So failing to change would turn away new sources of political energy and participation.

Escaping from mutual mistrust between leaders and led will demand changes of culture and behaviour at the top and the bottom. The new leadership needs to show it is prepared to engage, listen and to kick the 'control freak' tendency – with a willingness to be open to challenge, genuine dialogue and sometimes disagreement, treating those who have chosen to join the Party as grown-ups.

Party members should demand and be given a greater voice – and combine this with a willingness to take responsibility. When membership has fallen, those who are inside have a duty to ensure that we do not simply cling to what we know, in a way that could prevent the Party reaching out to involve people from all parts of society. Progressive parties, in government, need their members to remain impatient campaigners for further change. But that campaigning will only be effective when it engages with the reality of political change; not just making demands of government, but also building the support to make it possible, and resisting the temptation to indulge in headline-grabbing oppositionism.

This vision for Labour's future has deep roots in the Party's history and ethos. Just as in the US where the Republican right have been politically successful (although with disastrous policies) by mobilising a movement for change, the early Fabians and trade union movements offer examples from our own past. The Fabians created institutions, such as the Party itself, the LSE and *New Statesman*, and mobilised people through campaigns to replace the Poor Law with welfare and social justice, always educating, arguing and building new alliances for political change. We need to adapt these lessons to revive Labour as a progressive campaigning force today, energised by links with the new social and political movements of our own time.

In the run-up to a General Election, party reform will need to begin quickly. But the politics of 2007 are not those of 1994 to 1997. Change will be less effective and harder to sustain if simply unveiled and imposed from above. The newly elected Deputy Leader should make party reform their central task in the months ahead, engaging all parts of the Party in an open dialogue and using their mandate from members to seek to develop an agenda for change. The Party must urgently begin an honest and frank discussion about how Labour needs to change if it is again to lead the progressive political movements of the future.

“

1 | Why parties matter

A fashionable story dominates much public discussion of the problem with politics today. The electorate has become cynical and disaffected with formal politics because increasing educational attainment has allowed them to recognise just how out-of-touch and bankrupt politicians and parties are. Though apparently champing at the bit to get more involved, these 'new citizens' are therefore withdrawing from participation in formal politics and instead immersing themselves in community activism and campaigning groups. Yet the old parties and politicians – relics of a bygone age of class politics – maintain their selfish stranglehold on the system, preventing a new era of democracy from being born.

This was the broad thrust of the Power Inquiry, an independent Commission inquiry into Britain's democracy, published last year.[1] Its final report – *Power to the People* – gives voice to a variety of popular complaints: politicians are not listening and ignore what the people want; the parties lack principle and offer no choice to the electorate; and 'our system of electing parliamentary representatives is an obstacle to meaningful political involvement'.[2] If this is the problem, then the solution is obvious: change the institutions, change the parties, get the politicians in their place and put 'the people' in charge without having to work through the formal political structures… *et voila!* We will all come rushing back to engage in a new golden age of citizen democracy.

If only it were that simple. We believe this popular account needs to be challenged and rethought if we are to find an effective basis for democratic renewal. Here, we take the Power Inquiry as a central example simply because it clearly captures a great deal of the *zeitgeist* mood about what is wrong with politics today and how to fix it, seemingly taking at face value the sentiments which are common currency in the columns and letters pages of newspapers and on radio phone-ins.

Firstly, we observe that this account is at odds with some important evidence about political disengagement. A reform agenda based on a misdiagnosis of what is driving disengagement will have weak foundations.

The second problem is deeper: this account assimilates attitudes that reflect a profound misunderstanding of what politics is, and a denial of the necessary complexity of democratic decision making. 'Listen to the people' may be a popular slogan, but it is precisely because people disagree that we need politics to make collective decisions about our society as a whole.

Finally, while it is important that this defence of politics and political parties should find advocates across the political spectrum, we want to suggest that the rise of anti-politics harms progressive politics most of all, so fighting anti-politics is particularly urgent for Labour.

This is in no way a denial of the importance of political reform and renewal. Our central purpose in this pamphlet is to show why political parties – and Labour in particular – need to undertake significant cultural and organisational reforms if they are to reconnect with citizens. We also understand that attempts at re-engagement framed in terms of empowerment are more likely to go down better than ones framed in terms of, say, combating laziness – and in this respect, a certain amount of storytelling licence is surely justifiable. But they can only succeed if motivated by an honest understanding of the factors driving disengagement and disenchantment. Otherwise, there is a danger that such attempts risk contributing further to the very cynicism directed towards parties and politicians that is corroding our democracy.

Do people really hate the system?

Certainly, people do not like politicians much. The Hansard Society *Audit of Political Engagement* found that just 27 per cent of the public trusted politicians a great deal or a fair amount.[3] But there is little evidence of a golden age of political trust. Even at the height of the Second World War, Gallup found that only a third of citizens thought politicians were trying to do what was best for the country.[4]

Though the Power Inquiry reported a widespread sense that the main parties were at best, "failing" and, at worst, "an obstacle to meaningful engagement",[5] it is possible to overstate the level of anti-party sentiment among the public. Recent polling for the Young Foundation found that only 6 per cent of the public thought parties were bad for democracy (though worryingly a third thought they make no difference); by a margin of +23 per cent they rejected the idea that we would be better off if parties did not exist and all politicians were independent.[6] Similarly, the 2004 State of the Nation Poll found huge majorities agreeing that parties represent important strands of public opinion and give voters the opportunity to choose between different sets of policies.[7]

Indeed, despite the Inquiry's claim that participation in formal democracy "seems to provoke a unique distaste amongst British citizens", there is some evidence that satisfaction with democracy increases at election time. The immediate post-election survey of the 2005 British Election Study found that, by a margin of +40 (69 per cent to 29 per cent), people were satisfied with "the way democracy works in this country" (up from +33 before the election, and up from +31 in 2001).[8]

Nor are the kinds of pressure politics that have become increasingly prominent in recent years necessarily an alternative to conventional democratic involvement for participants. Most of those who are active in non-traditional political activities – from signing petitions to attending demonstrations – do so in addition to voting rather than as an alternative to it.[9] And survey data across countries shows that membership of voluntary organisations is a strong predictor of party membership.[10]

Is cynicism really a sign of enlightenment?

Though cynicism has grown at the same time that education levels in society have improved, at the individual level there is evidence that cynicism decreases with higher educational attainment. Recent studies have suggested that trust in politicians and Parliament increases with education – and that the cynicism gap between those with and without higher education grew between 1997 and 2001.[11]

It is also common to find positive effects of political knowledge on trust. When asked by the *Audit* how well MPs do their job, the public gave them a net rating of -7; but gave their own MPs an average rating of +29. As with public services, people's positive local perceptions are more likely to be grounded in concrete experience, while their views about the national picture are more likely to be formed through the media. Those who knew the name of their MP were also more likely to trust politicians in general.[12] As the *Audit* puts it, "greater knowledge seems to promote only positive, and not negative, reactions".[13]

Is there really a huge appetite for more political involvement?

Many people express the desire to have more say in political decisions. But probing beneath the surface reveals a big gap between this desire and what people are actually prepared to do.

The recent *Audit*, for example, found that signing a petition was the only activity that a majority of us would be willing to undertake to express a view on an issue of importance to us. Where more effort is needed, the appeal diminishes. Only a third said they would write to an MP, councillor or newspaper; and less than one in five would present their case at a public enquiry or take part in a governmental consultation (which might give pause to the most enthusiastic proponents of more direct participation). On top of this, the *Audit* found that, in practice, we do

What factors, if any, prevent you from getting more involved in politics?	%
Top four reasons chosen	
Lack of time / too busy / other commitments / priorities	32
Not interested / lack inclination / apathy / laziness / can't be bothered / lack of motivation	22
Disillusioned / cynical / politicians are untrustworthy	6
Wouldn't achieve / change anything / make a difference / waste of time	6
Other	
Wouldn't be heard / listened to	2
Unhappy with party / electoral system	2
Parties are all the same / don't represent my views	1
Don't know	17

Source: The Electoral Commission and Hansard Society, *An Audit of Political Engagement 4*

rather less than we think we might. Even for 'self-initiated' activities, such as contacting an MP or councillor, only around half of those expressing a willingness to do so had ever got round to doing it.

When asked why they do not engage more, many people were refreshingly honest – indeed, it was striking just how few people blamed the system rather than themselves (especially as respondents were allowed to choose multiple reasons). As the *Audit* concludes, "the most widespread obstacle to greater activism, then, is apparently neither hostility to politics nor a complete dismissal of its value, but a low assessment of its importance by people who perhaps might be more active were it a higher priority for them".[15]

We believe that the political system should be made more responsive, and that finding new ways of reaching out to people and communities is a crucial task for party reform. But the evidence shows that this will be hard work. We should not overestimate people's desire to participate. If institutional failure is not the primary cause of a lack of engagement, creating new modes of participation will not by itself change people's behaviour over the long term.

Misunderstanding politics

The popular narrative about disengagement is often at odds with the facts. But a deeper concern is the failure to understand – or perhaps a wilful refusal to confront – the complexity that is inherent in collective decision making. Below we look at three common examples. In each case, phenomena that are not only essential but also signs of politics doing exactly what it is supposed to are viewed by complainants as examples of politics going wrong.

1) Politics is about other people too

The rise of 'new citizens' is identified by the Power Inquiry as the driving force behind political disaffection. This more educated and sceptical citizenry expect individual choice and an adequate response from businesses and public services, and "there is no reason why the state and elected representatives should be any different".[16]

Except that the democratic state must be different. My individual self-interest can be sovereign when I go shopping as a consumer, but it has to be reconciled with other people's interests when I take part in collective decision making as a democratic citizen. As Meg Russell puts it in *Must Politics Disappoint?*, "politics does not allow everyone to get what they want". Democracy demands is that all interests are fairly taken into account, not that all are satisfied. Failing to recognise the difference between consumerism and politics by blurring "the spheres of citizenship and private individual gain" will create expectations "which are doomed to fail" and "can only feed disappointment in politics and the political".[17]

As Paul Webb observes, the failure to understand that politics cannot always give you what you want can give rise to a related perception: that just because you do not get what you want, you have not been listened to.[18] Yet if getting what you want is the benchmark for being listened to, then we have a problem since democratic politics can never deliver this – no matter how much listening is done – unless all citizens happen, magically, to agree.

2) 'The people' disagree

It is possible to acknowledge that other people have interests too and yet still evade political complexity – by claiming that everybody agrees. The Power report's contributors, for example, complain about politicians not "implementing what people actually want". The report laments the "ability of political power in Britain so easily to stonewall public demands"; and there is the related demand that MPs should more reliably "act as the voice of their constituents in Parliament".[19]

But just who is 'the public' here, and what are their 'demands'? Should MPs act as the voice of those in favour of the policy in question, or those against? All these comments buy into a fallacy of popular consensus on issues – as if somehow 'the people' are united in what they want and the political class is somehow failing to act on it. This is a key rhetorical device of populism – not only used to define citizens in opposition to politicians, but also to confer legitimacy on the views of individual complainants.[20]

There is also a tendency to overstate political consensus by focusing on those broad propositions on which we can all agree – which can in turn lead people to undervalue political negotiation.[21] Very few people are against less crime or a strong economy. So why can't the politicians stop bickering and get on with delivering what we all want? Because there will be intense disagreement about how to achieve these goals. Take the current 'consensus' on climate change. Certainly, agreement on emissions reduction targets marks important progress. But the real politics comes in the further debate – how will the targets be met? What type of market interventions and distortions are necessary? To what extent should people pay for the costs of their resource use? Achieving consensus on these questions would be an altogether different proposition.

3) Different issues might be related
Another common complaint is that parties are too 'broad brush', requiring support for broad programmes of policies, whereas campaign groups are "much more focused and require only that an individual supports change in one area".[22]

But decisions do need to be made across the whole range of policies, and those taken in one area will have consequences for others, either because they directly impinge on each other, or compete for limited financial resources, or need to be negotiated together. What's more, spelling out your intentions in advance across a range of issues affords some degree of electoral accountability. An MP elected to save Kidderminster hospital still has to choose how to vote on everything else. While that is of course his right, it is not entirely clear that his constituents were better off for him standing on a single-issue platform. Finally, political parties approach policy formulation on the basis of values and principles which, being abstract, recommend policy positions across a large range of areas. This is presumably why we are increasingly seeing 'single-issue' groups linking campaigns with similar value-orientations – addressing, for example, both international poverty and climate change.

Indeed, not only are the trade-offs, compromises and prioritisations between different policy decisions practically necessary, given the lack of public consensus on issue prioritisation, they are also morally virtuous. They ensure that different groups are taken into account and that interests are balanced.[23] But from a single-issue perspective, such compromises can be (and sometimes are) presented as morally dubious – as selling out on your principles.

The examples examined here all lend weight to Gerry Stoker's claim that increased discontent can partly be explained by a misunderstanding of the political process.[24] There is a danger that dissatisfaction with a political outcome is imagined to be the result of a failure of political process. When encountered, we need to challenge these misunderstandings rather than pandering to them and pretending we can construct a real-world politics based on them.

Anti-politics, democratic renewal and the left

The need for a defence of politics and parties should find support across the political spectrum. But we believe that anti-politics poses a particular threat to parties of the left. A willingness to recognise that others have needs and to accommodate their interests with yours underpins not just democratic politics, but also the legitimacy of the public realm itself.

We accept the frustrations of collective decision making not only because some public goods – like national defence and clean air – have to be provided collectively; as citizens, we have developed a consensus on enshrining some core values and principles for our society, for example, that health care should not depend on the ability to pay.[25]

There is a danger, therefore, that cynicism about collective decision making will undermine support for collective provision. This is why some on the British right, who argue for a smaller state, seek to use anti-politics to drive anti-statism. Indeed, a detailed and candid account of how anti-politics could help to roll back the state was published shortly after the 2005 election by a group of newly elected Conservative MPs and researchers (including those close to David Cameron).

> "The single most important component in the [US] Republicans' success is something that the British right could mimic, namely their determination to articulate the electorate's disdain for politicians and functionaries. A series of 'anti-politics' policies, ranging from term limits for legislators to limitations on budgets, helped establish in the public mind that at least some Republicans were with 'us' against 'them' – with, that is, the country against its *apparat*. This, above all, is what the British Conservatives need to do."[26]

This proposal for the Tories to "tap into anti-politician feeling" was not simply designed to gain tactical advantage against an incumbent government, however; it was about taking "our stand on the defence of the individual against the state" and promoting the idea that "the citizen should be as free as possible from state coercion".[27] The policy agenda flowing from this included many familiar themes, including replacing the NHS with a system of social insurance.

So as the party that believes that by the strength of our common endeavour we achieve more than we achieve alone, the Labour Party has a particular stake in fighting this type of anti-political sentiment. This does not mean a defence of 'old politics' against 'new politics', but an understanding of how reform must build from some central truths about democratic politics. Making politics work depends on institutions which engage in the aggregation of different interests and not only the insistent articulation of different demands.

Parties and elected representatives not only fulfil essential linking and accountability functions in our democracy, but act as key sites for conducting these processes of deliberation and conflict resolution in a representative fashion. The question is not whether we need parties, then, but how to reform them to better reconnect with citizens, and it is to this task that we now turn.

There are no magic bullets for fighting anti-politics. Relatively simple things could make a big difference, such as government and parties seeking to provide more feedback about how citizens' input has influenced decisions or being more open about the compromises that have to be made rather than presenting decisions as the best of all possible worlds.

Perhaps the single change which would have most long-term impact would be to use citizenship education and other parts of the curriculum to ensure that students leave school with a sounder understanding of the nature of democratic debate. This would involve less teaching about the history of Parliament or how local government is funded and more focus on understanding the processes of negotiation, conflict resolution, and trade-off that underpin collective decision making, as well as the true extent of diversity that exists in public opinion. Alongside this, students should develop a critical understanding of the media's reporting of the political process.

2 | Our approach to party reform

In anticipation of a change of Labour leadership, people have been talking about party renewal for some time now. But beyond the idea that it has to be done, no one can seem to agree on what 'renewal' requires the Party to do. Certainly people take the same starting points – a decline in poll ratings, party morale and party membership – but seem to end up with different conclusions on a bewildering array of subjects.

Some of this is simply down to differing analysis. Those who think that Labour is down in the polls because the Party is dangerously right-wing propose moving left as the solution; those who think it is because Labour is losing swing voters to the Tories propose an ever closer hugging of the centre. Similarly, for some, the decline in membership has been a dramatic collapse attributable to a 'Blair effect'; for others, it is simply that the 'Blair effect' which increased membership dramatically in the mid-1990s, has worn off, leaving the figures back on a trend of long-term historical decline.

However, much of it, especially when the argument comes around to issues of party structure or constitution, is nakedly instrumental – the result of a wilful confusion of means and ends. As Meg Russell has documented, there is a long history of instrumentalism in reform debates within the Labour Party, both on the left and the right.[1] In the late 1990s, when it looked as if One Member One Vote (OMOV) would not result in the selection of the leadership's preferred candidates as Welsh Party leader and London mayoral candidate, the requirement for unions to ballot their members was dropped; meanwhile, the left of the Party reversed its previous opposition and started insisting on the principles of OMOV.

Similarly, far too many current arguments are driven by a desire to re-engineer the power balance within the Party in favour of one group or another, rather than an honest analysis of the facts. Too many people are using debates about party reform to make proposals that are really about policy or to defend entrenched interests.

Though we understand how discontent has arisen from the way in which the leadership sometimes handles party procedure, in our view these defensive tendencies often underpin complaints heard today from the activist left. Whether on policy or procedure, a group of people claiming ownership of the true 'Labour' point of view are angry that the Government is pursuing policies with which they disagree. From this perspective, membership decline is seen as a consequence of these policies and the perceived abandonment of Labour values; the answer is for activists like them to "regain control of our party".[2] The resulting defensiveness can produce a rather territorial mindset, and a wariness about the engagement and involvement of a wider range of people ("What did we have to sacrifice to have these people in our tent?" was how Compass Chair Neal Lawson recently pondered the emergence of New Labour).[3]

These arguments are no doubt made in good faith, but in our view they are wrong (and not just because they imply a romanticised view of the past). The reality is that the long-term challenges that Labour now faces – declining participation and declining partisanship – are down to profound social changes that parties across all advanced industrial democracies are struggling to come to terms with. This is not to imply complacency; on the contrary, these challenges will require parties to work harder than ever before to retain support. But while there are of course aspects of Labour's situation that are down to specific policy decisions, pinning the blame on – and orienting reform around – relatively short-term aspects of our situation risks missing the point and allowing further decline.

How the world has changed

There is no shortage of accounts of how society has changed in the last 30 years. Fuelled by a cocktail of increasing affluence, rapid economic restructuring, deep changes in the patterns of family life and increasing access to choices that were not available to previous generations, Britain has become a more dynamic and open place. But it has also become more fragmented and less rooted. Economic change, geographical mobility and increasing individualism have helped to break the traditional bonds of class and community. While opportunity has risen, social cohesion has declined. Trust has fallen too – and not just in politicians: the number of adults agreeing that most people can be trusted fell from 56 per cent in 1959 to 45 per cent in 2000.[4]

Changes in associational behaviour

These changes have significantly affected citizens' associational behaviour and tastes in political engagement. Mirroring increased control and 'self-authorship' in other areas of life, people have come to demand more choice, voice and variety in their political activity and an immediate sense of efficacy, leading to an increasing rejection of one size fits all forms of participation. A less deferential citizenry is increasingly dissatisfied with representative forms of participation and does not necessarily accept that its relationship with an organisation should be mediated through others. Alongside this, the faster pace of life has left many with a sense of struggling to catch up: whereas 30 years ago money was considered people's most scarce resource, by 2005 they placed the highest value on time and energy.[5] These time pressures have put a premium on convenient and 'low-investment' activities, and those prepared to invest the kind of effort demanded by traditional political activism are an increasingly atypical minority.

As a result, all forms of associational behaviour which rely on collectivism have suffered. The decline of membership within the Labour Party – from a million members in the 1950s to 200,000 today – mirrors that in other political parties and civic associations (such as trade unions or the Women's Institute), both within the UK and elsewhere. The 2003 Citizen's Audit found that although much political activity still exists in Britain, it consists mainly of individual actions such as donating money or consumer boycotting, rather than collective actions like protests or strikes.[6]

Meanwhile, new forms of association have sprung up. The internet has given rise to new networks and communities. And the competitive landscape for parties has been transformed by the emergence of single-issue groups who offer a low-investment, high-feedback form of engagement which allows people to define themselves. Oxfam, for example, has almost doubled its membership over the last six years. Labour's monopoly of the progressive cause – if it ever existed – has long been broken; not only has what people want from participation changed, but there are now plenty more progressive organisations out there prepared to offer it.

The erosion of partisan loyalties

Perhaps the deepest impact of these economic and social trends on our politics, however, has been through gradual erosion of traditional voter loyalties. Whether measured by declining party identification or the declining vote share of the main parties, it is clear that partisan attachment has become weaker and more fickle. At the aggregate level, economic development has driven changes in class structure, which in turn has led to a shrinking of the main parties' natural support base. On top of this there has also been a more general de-alignment of party support within classes. At the individual level, meanwhile, this trend has been reinforced by a decline in party identification – the degree of psychological attachment to a particular political party – and a resultant volatility in citizens' voting behaviour. Those expressing very strong attachment to a party in the UK declined from 48 per cent in 1964 to 14 per cent in 2001.[7]

All these changes have led to a growth in the 'available' electorate, stimulating more aggressive party competition for these votes. And the way in which parties have responded to this increased vulnerability has been pretty consistent across different countries: they have transformed themselves more and more into centralised and professional campaigning organisations in which the leadership has increasing autonomy over party strategy.[8] Far from being a 'New Labour power-grab', the recent direction of reform within Labour has been mirrored by other parties in the UK and elsewhere.

And there are perfectly good reasons why. Confronted by a shrinking base of core voters and a more volatile electorate, parties have been obliged to break out of simply appealing to one section of the electorate as their natural support base and to campaign more intensively; as Mair and colleagues put it, parties have learned to move from "relying on a vote of belonging" to "campaigning for a vote of opinion".[9] Parties have therefore had to work harder on electoral strategy and to place as much emphasis on listening to voters as listening to their base. The increasing volatility of political preferences, with vote choice susceptible to the short-term considerations of an election campaign, means parties have had to become more responsive to emerging circumstances, reinforcing

21

the need for greater leadership autonomy. Add in a national 24 hour rolling media that requires parties to project their identity centrally and respond to events immediately and it is not difficult to see why all parties have moved closer to the status of centralised machines which are organised in a far more top-down way. The need for clear strategy, leadership autonomy, and faster response times, has required parties to build up their central staffing levels, professionalise their organisations and reform internal bureaucratic structures that slow down their ability to respond.

The truth is that many of the reforms that Labour underwent during the 1990s have been necessary for the Party to operate successfully in this changing electoral landscape. In particular, widening the franchise through OMOV (and, in doing so, reducing the likelihood of faction-alism) and moving to a deliberative style of policy making (and away from an adversarial resolution-based system) through the National Policy Forum (NPF) were not only improvements in principle, but have ensured that the leadership can operate without the same kind of debil-itating intra-party conflict as in the 1980s. That is not to deny that the way some of these reforms have been implemented has been without problems. The strangulated tone of some debates, insufficient ministe-rial engagement in the policy making process and too few opportunities for members to make their views heard are all problems which the next stage of party reform needs tackle. But there is no sense in which we can turn back the clock. In today's volatile electoral land-scape, parties must have key elements of centralisation and profession-alism in order to survive.

How to respond? Two challenges for Labour

This new model, however, has not been without its own dangers. There is a risk that, unless there is sufficient engagement and meaningful opportunities for participation, a party's membership and supporter base will wither away. Indeed, the needs of modern campaigning plus the decline in membership have led some to a counsel of despair, arguing that the Party just needs to bite the bullet and go to a virtual organisation, aimed solely at professional campaigning and election-eering. In a world where people's allegiances are looser and their appetite for traditional activism is much lower, they argue that there is little future in membership parties.

We do not share this view, and not just because members constitute a crucial source of pressure for progressive change, nor because they provide vital benefits to the Party, such as finance, ideas, volunteering and legitimacy. The fact is that exactly the same trends that make top-down organisation so vital in key areas also make a broad and engaged grassroots essential. Having strong links into communities is increas-ingly critical to give parties the kind of presence and responsiveness needed to win in a volatile electoral landscape – and the absence of such links makes a party particularly vulnerable to short-term shifts in public allegiance (as can be seen when a party loses its councillor base in an area). As the electorate becomes more fragmented and more fickle, parties must become better at listening to its different voices effectively and engaging directly with people who want to be listened to. And given the importance of face to face contact in political persuasion, a grassroots network can clearly play a vital role in diffusing progressive arguments, particularly in the face of a hostile media. So a diverse and vibrant base of participants is critical for keeping a party grounded and in touch with the concerns of the electorate. As the experience of the Tories' membership collapse of the 1990s showed all too clearly, a party that loses a broad membership base will often go on to lose its mind.

However, it is clear that participation in today's world cannot just mean traditional activism. As our polling – examined later – shows, many people simply do not want that and trying to build a plan for renewal around an attempt to resurrect a form of civic participation that has been falling out of favour for the last forty years seems doomed to failure. Instead, the Party needs to find a way of supporting and working with the different patterns of participation seen today. So the first challenge is to come up with new modes of participation that best reflect people's changing preferences while simultaneously allowing for effective leadership and the increased professionalisation needed to continue to perform effectively.

Secondly, while the growth in the 'available' electorate and the increased volatility in voting behaviour has put a premium on parties' ability to react to their changing electoral environment, it also gives them the opportunity to try and exert more control over this environment through actively shaping public opinion and building long-term support.

Voters' preferences, of course, are not a fixed aspect of the electoral system in which parties compete; parties can shape such preferences, as well as accommodating them. Much research here has tended to focus on the use of government power in shaping preferences, particularly through policies that manipulate the structure of the electorate and create new groups of support,[10] though evidence of the effectiveness of particular strategies is mixed.[11]

In this pamphlet, however, we will look at how parties can more proactively manage their electoral environment by using the main avenue open to them: political advocacy and persuasion. Indeed, the erosion of partisan loyalties not only gives parties an opportunity, but also creates a powerful incentive to try and shape voter preferences since over the long term this will offer greater security and sustainability than simply developing the means to respond to electoral volatility.

Finally, though we have framed these two challenges in terms of

Labour's sustainability, they are also crucial for its performance success. Too often we conceive of success narrowly in terms of winning elections. The Labour Party's defining mission should be to achieve maximum long-term progressive change. Winning elections is a crucial part of this, of course, as it enables the exercise of government power. But it is not the only part. Shaping public opinion is another key way in which parties achieve progressive change, not only because of its electoral value, but also because it influences individual and social action and is the best guarantee of ensuring progressive change endures. Direct action is a third way in which parties can achieve change – and this requires healthy participation. Pension Credit, the Cleaner Neighbourhoods Act and Sure Start are the products of progressive government action; but a local party leading a Pension Credit take-up campaign, clearing a local park or protesting against a Tory council's Sure Start cuts are also key elements of progressive politics.

So not only are shaping public opinion and increasing participation important in ensuring Labour's sustainability; they are both important objectives in their own right. And while the Party is pretty good at electioneering, these other two are both areas where it needs to raise its game. It is towards tackling these challenges that we turn in the next two chapters.

3 | Boosting participation

Labour has only ever prospered when it has drawn strength from the most dynamic currents in civil society.

David Miliband
Speech to the Fabian Society
December 2004

Creating a wide and active base of participants will ensure the Labour Party can compete successfully in the long term. But this is easier said than done. People seem less willing than ever before to commit or make the effort. Why should Labour be able to buck the trend?

In this chapter, we will argue that it is possible for the Labour Party to combine increased participation with the professional central organisation required for electoral survival if it embraces a more flexible and more personalised model of participation. Building on extensive polling of party and Non Governmental Organisation (NGO) activists and interviews with major advocacy groups, we will argue that Labour can not only boost its levels of participation, but also draw in the much broader mix of people the Party needs if it is to improve its effectiveness as a face to face campaigning organisation. The Party can accomplish this by learning from the experience of the most successful NGOs, and by offering supporters activities that appeal more to their interests, take more account of the external pressures they face, are effectively managed and, critically, make them feel more valued and listened to.

Increasing participation will involve getting better at matching what the Party needs to what potential participants want. To understand how this can be achieved, it is first worth exploring what the Party needs members and other participants for, and what potential members and participants want.

What does the Party need from participation?

Some of the traditional functions of members within the Party continue to be of supreme importance. Members provide finance and a critical campaigning resource of volunteers. Through their very existence, they provide the Party with legitimacy and continuity and serve some important anchoring roles, rooting the Party firmly in the distinctive values and beliefs of the left.

Along with these traditional roles, the social changes outlined in Chapter 2 mean that the Party will need members and other participants to play some newer – and potentially very different – roles. Critically, these new roles may require a more diverse mix of people to perform them.

In a more volatile electoral landscape, where understanding public concerns is increasingly important, members and other participants must provide a vital link to the public and be an effective sounding board for gauging their concerns – particularly important for Labour, as a party that seeks to act as a voice for ordinary working people. In a world where traditional forms of political communication, including the press, are ever less trusted, and voters put increasing faith in key intermediaries, it is clear that members and other participants will have to take up the challenge of acting as on the ground influencers. This will only work if the party can draw in respected local figures, for example, community leaders and public sector workers, who will act as ambassadors. Partisan erosion and electoral de-alignment also suggest the importance of members and other participants acting as 'bridgeheads', providing connections with new constituencies that allow the Party to extend its appeal and reach out to new groups.

All of these imperatives add up to one thing. The Party needs a model of participation that does not just attract more people, but attracts different kinds of people. It must become better at recruiting and retaining traditional activists. But it must also become much better at drawing in new types of participants, from a variety of backgrounds, and with different personal objectives, to play these newer roles. More of the same on its own will not solve the problem and, as our polling shows, is also not a viable offer for many potential participants.

While political parties have languished and many traditional forms of civic association have seen their memberships dwindle, campaigning NGOs have experienced a boom. For instance, since the early 1980s, four of the leading environmental NGOs have seen their collective membership triple at the same time as the main political parties have seen their participation rates drop.[1] They have done this while maintaining tight professional organisation.

This is not to say that parties should, or even could, try to emulate NGOs wholesale. Given Labour's democratic nature and representative structures, members of course have a different status within, and relationship to, the Party than exists in most NGOs. And the two organisations play very different roles in the political system. Nevertheless, an effective model of party reform should engage with the work NGOs have undertaken in this area and look for possible lessons.

The lessons of the NGO model

The models of NGO membership and organisation vary, but the NGOs we profiled seem to have a number of crucial elements in common.

1) A variable model of participation

NGOs provide highly varied participation opportunities to ensure there is something for everyone. They offer multiple levels of association that reflect people's diverse preferences and expectations. Participation can be purely symbolic in terms of subscribing to email updates or wearing a white band; it can be purely financial; or it can involve more time-intensive volunteering commitments. Oxfam, for example, recognise five different levels of association, from sporadic donor to super-activist. Of their approximately one million members, only about 2,000 are categorised as at the high end of activism, a very small proportion overall. Critically, each rung of activity is seen as an end in itself.

In addition, many NGOs set low entry barriers to participation and make low levels of contribution rewarding. Oxfam provide an easy first step towards participation that is valued both for its own worth and for the potential it has to be built on, at a pace to suit the individual. Their 'I'm in' campaign has a minimal initial ask – declare your intention to change the world by signing up to an email alert, and you explicitly become part of the global movement to end poverty – a grand claim for such a small action. In particular, NGOs often seek to engage people through specific campaigns rather than general organisational member-ship. 'Make Poverty History' is just the most well known example of how NGOs used a high profile, highly focused campaign to engage people and draw them into participation and action.

2) Investing in people

The NGOs we examined invest heavily in strengthening their organ-ising base and the professionalism of their volunteer and member management. Many leading NGOs use well trained and rigorously managed local managers to focus on making the volunteer experience a satisfying one. This directly leads to better rates of recruitment and retention among members. The National Trust, for example, has prioritised investment in, and performance management of, local middle management. This is key to identifying a volunteer's needs and experience and then matching them to appropriate roles. This has been combined with investment in new technology to ensure that contact with members is as satisfying and as tailored as possible. Volunteers are well trained and there is a high benchmark for quality: volunteering does not have to equate to amateurism. This strategy is considered crucial to the success of the Trust, which places a high value on retaining satisfied volunteers. This illustrates an important, and somewhat paradoxical, point: effective national organisation and performance management is necessary for a thriving local base.

3) Central organisation – local autonomy

These organisations combine relatively tight central organisation and leadership with significant room for local autonomy and campaigning. Indeed, unlike parties, most NGOs have minimal internal democratic accountability, yet combine this with wide scope for local activist autonomy and initiative, which allows grassroots activity to flourish in parallel. Individual local groups operate under the organisational banner, but with considerable potential for their own campaigning and creativity. The overall identity is structured loosely. For example, for Friends of the Earth the sense of being part of an environmental justice movement is more important than members having to sign up to the entire organisational line. NGOs tend to allow a porousness and flexibility of opinions while providing a clear value proposition that people of different views can coalesce around.

4) Valuing participation

Finally, the NGOs we examined maintain high levels of satisfaction and participation by making each participant feel valued and personally efficacious. Our polling shows that 71 per cent of NGO members and 67 per cent of Labour members felt they had little or no power to influence their organisation's position. Yet 81 per cent of NGO members thought their membership contributed to the organisation's ability to achieve its aims and 74 per cent felt their contribution was recognised and valued – significantly higher than the figures of 62 per cent and 52 per cent, respectively, for Labour Party members.

Our evidence suggests that two things lie behind this. Firstly, NGO members feel listened to: 73 per cent of NGO members we surveyed felt their organisation listens to their views in deciding its position on issues, as opposed to only 55 per cent of Labour Party members. While the organisations offer them little formal say in policy or campaign choices, they make them feel they have a voice and are in a discursive relationship. Some of this may be a consequence of the activity of NGO participation itself, which is inherently expressive. But much of it also reflects the extent to which the organisations explicitly solicit opinions and offer members a voice in the process, even if this ultimately does not determine outcomes. Secondly, the strategy of the NGOs we profiled involves welcoming all contributions and emphasising their impact. Every contact with participants is used to reinforce a consistent message of external political efficacy and to convey a vision and a message of hope.

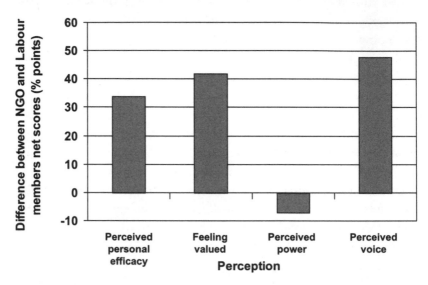

The Labour Party has taken steps to respond to contemporary challenges of participation, for instance, through the establishment of the Labour Supporters Network (LSN). But supporters are seen by many involved primarily as 'members in waiting'. Membership remains focused on the traditional one size fits all model of participation, which sets very high barriers to entry. Members are asked to sign up to the Party on an all-or-nothing basis, where the only distinction is between the active and the inactive. Standard participation activities entail time- and energy-intensive commitments. In a world where many people feel pressured and time constrained, this lack of flexibility may be scaring off many potential participants.

Our polling suggests that to encourage current Party members to increase their levels of participation, the activities and opportunities offered must be more convenient, more efficacious and more relevant to

Labour's beliefs and values.[2] To draw people in who are not currently members, there is a priority on building and diversifying the issue-based campaigning the Party offers and offering projects that are relevant to local communities.[3]

How Labour should change its approach to participation

If Labour is to learn from the success of NGOs in sustaining participation, the implications are clear: the Labour Party must build a more fluid and flexible model of participation, and focus on providing a 'personalised' form of activity that chimes with what people want and expect. Such a 'variable model' of participation is not only more attractive to people, but would also reflect the multiple functions the Party needs members and supporters to perform.

This will entail a mixture of strengthening current systems to maximise the impact of traditional members and activists, while simultaneously creating different levels of association. The LSN and Let's Talk are a starting point, but the Labour Party must go radically further. Alternative modes of participation must be developed – for example, campaigning or discussion groups within the Party, open to non-members, that can coexist with more traditional forms of activism. Reform will fail if it is based on the expectation that people will make the leap from apathetic to activist overnight. Instead, it must focus on developing the intervening shades of grey to encourage a valuable first dip into the Labour movement. Given the benefits for the Party of even the lowest investment participation, this initial contribution must be valued for its own worth, and not just for its potential to deepen over time.

These are controversial issues that are hotly debated within the Party. However, our polling of the group which we regarded as the most likely to become involved with the Party (Labour-identifying NGO members and community activists who were not Party members) suggests that this more flexible approach to party involvement could yield significant dividends. As shown in the chart below, while just 9 per cent of the target group signalled a willingness to consider joining the Party as a full member, significantly higher numbers said that they would be prepared to be involved if a more flexible menu of options was available. 34 per cent indicated they would be willing to become a registered supporter, not paying a membership fee or having constitutional rights, but receiving information and invitations to events. 49 per cent would be willing to attend Labour Party events and debates in their area, without joining or registering for anything. The figures rose further when offered the prospect of simply signing up to a specific campaign: 59 per cent would be willing to support a Labour campaign on a specific national or international issue of concern; 51 per cent would be willing to support a campaign against a particular Conservative policy; and 64

Willingness to participate

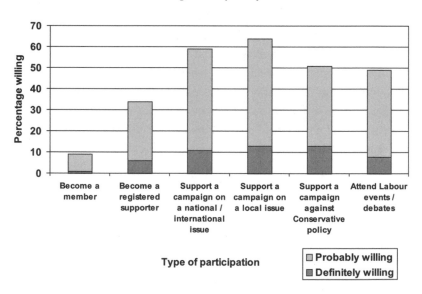

per cent would support a Labour campaign to achieve change in the local community – over seven times more than would be amenable to traditional membership.

Sustaining members and non-member participants alongside each other need not be problematic for the Labour Party. Other organisations manage the duality perfectly well. No one believes that a football club cannot have season ticket holders and passionate, but less committed supporters too, not to mention the fair weather friends. Season ticket holders give up more time, provide more financial support and enjoy greater access as a result. This does not stop supporters playing a valuable role, filling empty seats, providing legitimacy through numbers and playing an important advocacy role amongst their peers. Their support is broader and more flexible, but is important nonetheless. Where people are willing – even in the smallest way – to associate with the Labour Party, then the Party should offer them vehicles to express that aspect of their identity.

The Party should therefore seek to strengthen its issue campaigning role as a significant route into participation. Indeed, given that the Labour Party is an important site for pressure politics as well as democratic policy making, by creating constructive campaigns with active ministerial engagement, the Party could begin to compete with – or, alternatively, work in partnership with – other campaign groups. Nationally, the Party and its affiliate organisations should experiment with a variety of campaign themes that will draw people in and harness their energy around key sets of issues.

At local level, parties must be supported to run on-going campaigns focused on driving concrete change on pressing local issues. The Labour Party must step out of the meeting hall and into the community if it is to offer people an attractive movement to participate in. As part of this approach, local parties should be supported to build campaigning coalitions with other progressive organisations. This will entail giving local parties – just like local units of NGOs – a degree of autonomy over what they campaign on and how. That local responsiveness will be critical in permitting local parties to mould their approach to the demands of each constituency.

The Labour Party, both centrally and locally, must increase the number of opportunities for participation, as well as the quality of the participation experience. People who are willing to give up their time for the Party must be matched to appropriate activities and their contribution effectively managed and valued. This should involve widening and strengthening the organiser base, including through training, to ensure that all constituencies can benefit from high quality, if not professional, organisers who are assessed and overseen – but not controlled – by the central party. The range of local party activity and benchmarks for effective volunteer management should be explicit rather than implicit, and local parties should receive more central support to raise the impact and efficiency of their activities.

Critically, the Party needs to become better at offering members and supporters a greater sense of political efficacy. This could be as simple as relaying a message of thanks for a contribution to a campaign to highlight the role members played in achieving progressive outcomes. One of the most important lessons to be learnt from NGOs is that, both locally and nationally, the Party needs to work to embed positive feedback mechanisms into everything it does.

Practical steps also need to be taken to add to participants' sense of voice. As our evidence makes clear, this is not necessarily about changing power relations within the Party's internal democratic structures. Rather, it is about creating more open and genuine forums for debate. In the final chapter, we mention the importance of improving the National Policy Forum process to enhance the quality of discussion and debate for members. But in terms of forums for wider modes of participation, one possibility could be to extend and institutionalise the discursive model of Let's Talk, both involving members and new groups. These will need structured feedback processes built in to underpin their relevance and demonstrate effective input over the longer term. As we envisage it, these forums would not have any formal status with respect to the Party's policy platform, but they would play an important role in ensuring that all those within, and close to, the wider Labour movement feel heard and valued.

All these proposals represent a challenge not just for the organisation, but for the culture and the self-image of the Party. An important reason why the NGO model is successful is that it is wrapped up in a clear, value-based vision that motivates people to opt into a cause and engenders a sense of momentum towards change. They understand that they are competing with other organisations in the 'marketplace of idealism' and need to sell a positive vision of participation that arouses action. But for Labour, those activities that allow members to express values and beliefs are too often relegated to 'Any Other Business'.

Our polling suggests that a more values-based projection of the Party's identity and activities would constitute a more attractive offer, strengthening the commitment of current members and opening it up to newcomers. Crucial barriers to participation cited by the target group of Labour-identifying non-members are disagreement with the Party over particular policies and the feeling that association would constitute support for everything the Party does.[4] Enabling identifiers to associate with the Party in a looser sense, based on a shared commitment to core values, would open up the Labour movement beyond its current reach. To inspire hope, the Party must become better at articulating a vision of change and welcoming all members of the progressive family who share these broad objectives.

An 'engagement arm': implementing a 'variable model' approach to participation

Implementing a more flexible model of participation, with a variety of associational links, will present the Party with a significant challenge. It will of course require the buy-in of everyone in the Party to work. But some activists see such reform as a cynical attempt by the leadership to dilute the power of 'real' members and remain stubbornly wedded to the traditional forms of party organisation and participation. Jon Cruddas and John Harris, for example, give voice to this protectionist tendency in their recent pamphlet.[5] The LSN is "a systematic assault on Labour's basic federal structure"; "blurring" the definition of local parties "will only serve to hamper their work"; if a good number of members have left because of a perceived lack of say in the direction of the Party, they ask, "why address the problem via a new kind of membership that will have even less input?"

We have no doubt these arguments are made in good faith, but such views potentially form a barrier to the Party's ability to transform its relationship with a new generation of potential participants. We will need to reach out to involve many more people in Party activities, recognising – as our polling shows – that influencing the Party's position is not everyone's priority. When asked to pick some different activities that might encourage them to get involved, our target group of non-members ranked taking part in discussions and debates (24 per cent) above 'making my views heard within the party' (17 per cent) and taking part in the policy making process (13 per cent).[6]

In order to successfully implement a flexible model of participation, it must be explicit that the constitutional rights and roles of membership should reside only with 'full' members. Our suggestion for squaring this circle is simply to create a new 'engagement arm' of the Party, which sits outside constitutionally defined relationships, through which it can deliver the events and offer the forums for debate that a more flexible model of participation demands.

This would consist of a set of porous networks, along with both locally and nationally organised events, campaigns and other activities open to those not wanting full membership as well as to members. We envisage this new structure of participation involving an annual rhythm of national events around the country, local events following a national agenda in each region, and free-standing local events too – a 'permanent fringe'. There would be a dedicated unit within Party HQ for managing these modes of participation, rather than them simply being an add-on to the policy making process.

As we see it, national and regional staff would support local activity, helping local parties organise events and get party and non-party speakers. Indeed, delivering these activities on the ground would be a core function of the new set of local organisers we are envisaging, working with councillors and General Committees (GCs). Local parties would have access to non-member lists – with staff facilitating rather than hindering horizontal communication between different groups – though their use would be mediated by the Party to prevent abuse of the system. Similarly, unions, socialist societies and related non-affiliated organisations would be encouraged to organise and engage in these activities, just as they participate at the conference fringe. Again, the central Party's unit could act as a clearinghouse, providing access to non-member lists where appropriate.

Because they would have no constitutional significance, not only would these 'engagement arm' structures and activities avoid the dilution of membership status, but their establishment and running would also not be subject to activist veto. We envisage this type of non-member participation as a core part of the functioning of the Party, not just an add-on to normal GC activities. None of which is to say, of course, that we do not think that members would want to be involved in such activities; indeed, the success of such activities may well hinge on enthusiastic member involvement. In many cases it would be local parties themselves who would want to deliver the activities on the ground. But in cases where there was no desire to do this, local and regional organisers would deliver them outside of other local party activity.

Nor would the operation of such engagement activities be subject to the kind of internal bargaining processes that can so often hamper the Party's potential for public engagement. There is a reason why literature produced through the NPF is turgid and impenetrable – it is subject to a democratic amendment process. Liberating the Party to produce documents for political education and public engagement work outside of these bureaucratic arrangements is essential if it is to produce the high quality material that can inspire both members and non-members alike.

Of course, resourcing this new 'arm' of the Party would not be straightforward, but given the public engagement nature of many of the activities involved, we would hope that at least some of them – such as education, civic action, or debates and deliberative events – would be suitable candidates for any public funding available through impending reform of party funding.

Opening up

The issues discussed here are not just a challenge for the central party, which must reform its offer of participation, but for the existing activists too, who must become more accepting of diversity of involvement within their own ranks. If reform only seeks to address the needs of those already inside the Party, it will not address the challenge of opening up to attract new people. Local party activity must always be welcoming, even to those who do not pass the perceived litmus tests. Dedication to the cause cannot simply be measured in terms of meetings attended or leaflets distributed. The hope is that as members become more confident and satisfied with their own experience of participation, it will be perceived as less problematic if the boundaries between the membership and the wider public can become less stark.

4 | Shaping public opinion and building long-term support

We have to move this country in a new direction, to change the way we look at things, to create a wholly new attitude of mind.

Margaret Thatcher
Speech to Conservative Party Conference
12 October 1979

After ten years in power, Labour has had some real successes in shifting key debates in a more progressive direction. The Conservatives are now reluctant to tout tax cuts and are falling over themselves to promise extra investment in public services. Five years after proposing that it be replaced with a system of social insurance, David Cameron is telling everyone how much he loves the NHS. The country itself is becoming more socially liberal, with many Tories changing their stance on issues like gay rights.

Some of these changes, however, seem fragile – as if they could easily shift back again in future. Many of the Tories' accommodations are patently cosmetic. And it is unclear how entrenched key elements of Labour's programme are among the public. If the Tories came to power and wanted to abolish Educational Maintenance Allowances and equal rights for part-time workers, would it really be difficult for them?

Two disappointments stand out in particular. Firstly, Labour does not seem to have extracted durable political credit for some of its most popular policies. Despite the fact that Labour has made improving public service provision a priority, recent data from MORI found that the relationship between views of public services and views of government is weak, "so even if the public does notice that services are delivering, it may not directly improve their views of the government".[1] And if this is the case with public services, it feels all the more so with many other popular policies – like the campaign to make poverty history, for example. Despite public support for the Government's policies in these areas, the identity of those policies does not seem to have attached to Labour in a more fundamental way.

Secondly, where Labour's progressive policies have been popular, they have not been used as beachheads to further reinforce progressive values in the public mind and create space for further change. Extra financial support through tax credits is popular, but support for the principle behind it – progressive universalism – does not seem to have been embedded. The numbers supporting income redistribution have fallen from 50 per cent to 40 per cent in the decade to 2004, even though the number thinking the income gap is too big rose.[2]

Winning elections is of course absolutely necessary to deliver a real progressive shift in public opinion – only through repeated electoral success can a party hope to dominate the political agenda and force their opponents to adapt. But winning is not on its own sufficient. One only has to look at the ease with which the Republicans subsequently erased the progressive advances of the Clinton years to know that years in office – particularly if spent parroting rhetoric from the opposition – do not on their own produce shifts in the centre ground of politics. Something more is needed.

What that something may be, forms the focus of this chapter. First, we look at two examples of where political movements have successfully shifted the political centre: the US Republicans and the wider US conservative movement between the 1950s and the 1980s, and the UK anti-European movement. We then go on to look at what lessons may be learned for the Labour Party.

What successful examples tell us

The US Republicans and conservative movement in America from the 1950s to the 1980s

From the late 1950s onwards a conservative movement began to organise in the US that by the 1980s had utterly changed the terms of political debate – symbolised by a Reagan victory in 1980 on the same conservative platform that had led to crushing defeat for Barry Goldwater in 1964. At the heart of the Republicans' success was their ability to root arguments for policies in terms of highly resonant values of freedom, nationhood and moral traditionalism – such that to espouse them was to support Republican positions. Appeals to values and principles were used not only to reinforce support for policy positions, but were instrumental in driving underlying value change – in particular, leading to a marked decline in the weight Americans placed on the importance of equality.[3] Underpinning this was the development of strategic thinking about the consequences of demographic and social trends for the evolution of public opinion, most famously set out in Nixon adviser Kevin Phillips' tome *The Emerging Republican Majority* (1969), and how to capitalise on these through a set of campaigns framed around key issues and through the targeting of different constituencies in American society.

A crucial element of the Republicans' success during this period was the development of a rich network of advocacy and mobilising institutions. A rich set of right-wing think tanks, for example, the American Enterprise Institute, the Hudson Institute, the Heritage Foundation and the Cato Institute helped re-shape the country's political discourse, both providing a refuge for conservative intellectuals, and focusing their talents on a practical battle of ideas. Sympathetic parallel organisations with membership bases were used to spread the word at grassroots level and mobilise their potential supporter base, such as the Young Americans for Freedom on university campuses in the 1960s. Local organisation created a vigorous citizen activist base to build party support (one study has demonstrated that shifts in party support on race-centred issues in the 1970's were actually driven by citizen advocacy, rather than elite discourse[4]) and energy was channelled into recruiting influential local opinion formers, from businessmen to pastors. Underpinning all this was effective coordination between different actors or groups.

The UK anti-European movement since the 1980s

Over the last 15 years, the anti-European movement in the UK has shifted public opinion and hardened Eurosceptic sentiment to such a degree that even a popular pro-European prime minister with a three-figure majority felt unable to pursue his ambitions. Though Britain's anti-EU campaigns date back to the 1960s, it was not until the late 1980s that they began to blossom. A simple message rooted in populist values – sovereignty, freedom and nationalism – and supported by a Eurosceptic press, developed into a movement that by the millennium consisted of over 20 anti-EU and anti-EMU organisations, many working in sympathy with the Conservative Party. The movement has picked symbolic and strategic fights to create definition around key arguments and to drive the agenda, whether on the metric system, fishing policy or the EU rebate. The organisations themselves cover and target different key constituencies – everything from the British Housewives League to Business for Sterling. As well as trying to shape elite discourse, they have sought to mobilise people through local activism, such as the Democracy Movement's 'Democracy Days', replete with street stalls, pamphlets and newsletters.

The anti-European movement is a loose but co-operative network of overlapping groups, acting independently and with many different shades of opinion, but with key elements of co-ordination in campaigning – including with the Conservative Party and sympathetic media. This coordination is enhanced in part by the existence of umbrella groups at national level (the Campaign Against the European Constitution), and even at EU level (the European Alliance of EU-critical Movements). Co-ordination occurs mainly through cross-membership, with key figures sitting at the nexus of several organisations (whether parliamentarians, financiers, academics, etc.). Movement of staff between campaigns and organisations is also quite fluid.

*   *   *

Though these case studies are necessarily brief, they highlight several important factors in changing public opinion. First is political strategy and persuasion: value-based advocacy, framing and provoking debate, and building the necessary capacity to plan and execute this strategy over the long term. Second is the need for movements to develop a broad network of advocacy organisations that can shape specific debates, influence opinion-formers and give the movement maximum influence over key constituencies at grassroots level. The final point is cultural: these types of strategic approaches have worked because all the organisations within these movements have been able to combine a healthy pluralism and openness of tone with co-ordination and a constant focus on their primary shared goal.

Re-politicising policy
Making values explicit

One of the most important lessons from the success of the US conservative movement in driving opinion change is the necessity of value-based advocacy in political discourse. Superficially this was done by enhancing support for policies by rooting them in popular values. These values then acted as a heuristic to simplify the political discourse and guide voters' judgements. But it went far deeper than this, shifting public opinion by pro-actively building support for the conservative values themselves.

A good deal of research shows the importance of principles and values in structuring political attitudes – and that differences in how people weight a particular value, for example equality, give rise to differences in policy preferences, for example social welfare.[5] Building support for values and their associated political principles, then, is not only far more powerful than simply building support for specific policies; if successful, it makes possible a whole range of further policy action that follows from these values and principles. Thatcher's mantra of 'rolling back the state', for example, was not about any particular policy, but an attempt to embed her own libertarian conception of freedom.

But values and principles need to be made explicit in order to do this. This is why it is disappointing that there has been little value-based advocacy around some of Labour's most popular policies. Thanks to the Tories and the right-wing press, for example, regulation has a bad name, more likely to be associated with 'red tape' and government interference. Yet the right-wing tabloids – and the public more generally – loved the Government's extension of maternity leave and measures to outlaw dangerous toys. A more value orientated presentation of labour market regulation and consumer protection regulation could have helped drive underlying support for regulating markets for the protection of all, and for government power as a force for good more generally.

Making values explicit alongside the policies to which they give rise is also relevant to the other challenge outlined at the beginning of this chapter: how Labour can derive more credit from those policies that are popular. Branding a policy as 'Labour' is more than just the Labour Government doing it: it requires an understanding of why the policy itself is Labour and exclusively so. By revealing how the motivating force for the policy stems from your underlying principles – and not those of your opponents – you can brand the policy as naturally and exclusively yours.

Framing and provoking debate

The case studies also show the importance of picking strategic fights and then joining them. There is a plethora of evidence to show that political conflict 'activates' issues in public opinion, making people more likely to make judgements on the basis of an issue, and in some cases heightening the role of their partisan preferences in political choice.[6] In this way, provoking debate can solidify or weaken public support for particular agendas.

Success requires framing debates in a way that clearly defines your position against your opponent. The Government's record here has been both good and bad. In areas like public investment it has constructed some robust dividing lines, yet too often it has muddied the waters by framing its position in terms of internal party debates, such as over public service reform. There are also undoubtedly times when Labour has failed to exploit fully being on the popular side of some significant dividing lines – such as measures to extend flexible working rights in the 2002 Employment Act.

If value-based advocacy and the partisan presentation of policy are important in shaping public opinion and building progressive support, then a key aspect of renewing Labour in government will be a willingness to politicise policy more than it does at the moment. There is perhaps a sense in which Labour has been captured – or at least 'domesticated' – by the culture of government, where a growing surrender to the technocratic language of the civil service and the needs of stake-holder management has overridden the need to present policy in a more political way. Certainly there are moments for national unity across parties, but right now what we need is more of a battle of ideas – and this will require a re-injection of energy into Labour's political argumentation.

Building political and strategic capacity

The success of the US conservative movement also demonstrates the need to develop the capacity not only to execute political campaigns effectively, but also to plan them strategically over a number of years. The change of Labour leadership provides a good opportunity to start afresh and identify the long-term arguments we need to win over the coming years, and to define a series of political campaigns that will permanently shift the centre ground of British politics.

But Labour will need to build the central capacity to handle policy in a more political way, moving away from a reliance on government planning, and on official government material for policy presentation, and strengthening their capability to produce and execute political campaigns outside of departmental agendas. And as the Tories' policy commissions illustrate well, reclaiming the Party as a site for high-level activity is also important for liaising with national opinion formers: relationship building may have to happen in a departmental context if part of government business, but must also be pursued in a political context if it is to generate the kind of political capital the Party needs.

The need for multiple voices: advocacy networks

Shifting public opinion and building long-term support for the Party effectively require not only the right progressive arguments, but also appropriate networks for disseminating them – in particular, outward-facing parallel organisations and opinion formers that can work with parties to advance progressive arguments. Developing advocacy networks is urgently needed for Labour at this time. After ten years in government, it is hard to get people to give you a fair hearing. But they will listen to friends, community leaders, public sector workers, academic experts, campaign groups, and so on.

The Tories seemed to learn this lesson in the 2004 referendum campaign over an elected assembly for the North East. Knowing they had little support in the region, they used 'non-politicians' as the spokespeople for the 'No' campaign, from local businessmen to Eurosceptic market traders. When 'ordinary people' (as political activists were presented in this case) were pitted against 'politicians' and the establishment, many people clearly trusted the former. It is a lesson the Tories have seemingly taken to heart. These days, a government minister on the news is as likely to find himself up against a right-wing columnist or a Tory blogger as a Tory shadow minister.

Parallel organisations and opinion formers can potentially fill a variety of advocacy roles:

1) Framing debates

First, and perhaps most important, is setting the agenda by framing debates. Polly Toynbee has been incredibly successful in this regard, plugging away valiantly for years to set up a simple debate: you can either care about relative poverty or not, but you cannot claim to be very nice if you do not. It was this framing of the debate about poverty that compelled the Tories to say they identified with her last year.

2) Giving credit where credit is due

A second role is conferring legitimacy on individual policy decisions or endorsing the direction of travel, which is particularly important when the Government is under attack from the right. The shopworkers' union USDAW has been one of the most effective organisations at publicly endorsing progressive policies. The significant success it has had in influencing government policy over the years shows there is no contradiction between representing your members' interests through inward-facing lobbying and promoting progressive change through outward-facing advocacy.

3) Creating political space
A third role is creating space for policymakers to move into, by employing campaigns primarily to shape the context of political decision making, rather than the content – such as the way the Jubilee 2000 campaign mobilised people to constructively demonstrate public demand for further political action. While it is government's role to show leadership, it is also the case that reforms are more likely to be successful and endure if they respond, and are seen to respond, to public mobilisation.

4) Scrutinising opposition parties
Another role is scrutinising opposition parties, whether that is their policies, or their claims. Two excellent examples of the latter occurred prior to the 2005 election when the Tories were whipping up fear about violent crime. Firstly, an academic criminologist responded swiftly to Michael Howard with an article explaining why he was misrepresenting the statistics, and then a chief constable attacked the Tories for misleading the public – both devastating interventions from trusted 'non-political' voices.

Sadly, examples of progressive organisations filling these roles are notable only for their exceptionality. In practice, many seem to be purely inward-facing lobbying organisations that adopt an oppositional footing to extract policy concessions. They demonstrate little concern for how this might square with the electorate. Many academics, though progressive, are reluctant to enter political debates, and public sector workers are far too angry with the Government about public service reform to undertake this necessary work. (Note we are not claiming that any group should see its business as supporting the Labour Government *per se*, but that such groups can be instrumental in building progressive support in tandem with government, thereby helping to fulfil their broader organisational objectives.)

Indeed, when a recent UNICEF report argued the Government was failing children, using figures that were in some cases several years out of date, it was left to Michael Gove, a Tory shadow minister, to say the report "was actually unfair to the Government". Worse still, the negative and oppositional nature of many voices on the left can actively undermine both Labour's progressive achievements and its ability to argue the case by itself.

All in all, when the Labour Party and Labour Government are the only institutions making Labour arguments, we are in deep trouble; yet that is where we seem to be at the moment.

Think tanks and campaigning groups provide a marked example of the contrast between the willingness of those on the British left and right to engage in advocacy. Right-wing think tanks tend to be engaged less in policy development than in campaigning work and outward-facing propagation of conservative principles and beliefs. Those on the left, however, tend to pursue a more inward-facing kind of policy criticism and development. It is as if we have forgotten that directly influencing government is not the only way to achieve long-term progressive outcomes. Right-wing think tanks are also more coordinated, with some of them holding regular meetings that include shadow cabinet ministers, to explore how they can work together to promote Conservative principles and messages.[7]

It is uncertain how many organisations on the left see themselves as responsible for, or partners of, the Labour Party in the task of shifting public opinion leftwards. In many areas, campaigning groups understandably want to say the Government is failing because it has not gone far enough, but by not giving credit for the progress the Government has made, they risk inadvertently endorsing the message of the right, who want to say the Government is failing because it is going in the wrong direction. There is often a woeful failure of campaigning groups to effectively connect with their real opponents (in Spring 2007 you would search in vain, for example, for any reference to Ryanair on green groups' websites.)

So what has to change? As a priority, the Labour Party needs to reach out to its existing sister organisations and NGOs to see if, despite their differences, they can nevertheless work in partnership to campaign together on broader shared objectives. There is a need not only to challenge organisations on the left over their own contributions to driving opinion change through outward-facing campaigns, but also for Labour to take these organisations more seriously as partners in this endeavour, working alongside them on the content of campaigns not just at election times but in between too.

In many cases, however, we suspect this will prove difficult at best. The Government's relationship with trade unions, NGOs and other campaigning groups has broken down over issues of policy, despite their all sharing broader objectives to which the Conservatives are fundamentally hostile. And for representative organisations, representing their members' interests will in the short term often necessitate a government-facing stance.

What will be necessary, then, is for the left to seed new parallel institutions. Where, for example, is our counterpart to the Taxpayers' Alliance, scrutinising the Tories' commitment to shrinking the size of the state? The right has nurtured an effective set of advocacy organisations along key dividing lines, such as Migrationwatch on immigration or Civitas on family values. What the left needs is a similar set of outward-facing parallel institutions to frame its own debates: a Tory-facing campaign on employment rights, for example, could highlight the consequences of Cameron's pledge to withdraw from the Social Chapter.

Ultimately, political campaigning organisations need to be independently financed, and there are no magic bullets here, though such 'organisations' do not necessarily cost much to start up. An examination of experience elsewhere has shown that key individuals can play an important role in linking others with shared interests, in fundraising, and in matching finance with appropriate investment opportunities. This is an area where developing the right strategic capacity within the Party could involve someone to catalyse the growth of, and coordinate with, such organisations.

It is not just parallel organisations that the Party needs to develop to undertake this important campaigning and advocacy work. Given the importance of informal networks in creating and reinforcing political support, it is obvious that the Party needs to focus more on individual and local advocacy.[8] We believe there is a substantial appetite amongst local parties, members and supporters for more active engagement in making progressive arguments – an appetite which could be harnessed much better if they were provided with the right information, tools and opportunities. Our polling showed the target group of non-members are especially attracted by campaigning: in addition to campaigns on local issues, the activity that the largest number of Labour-supporting non-members we polled said they would definitely get involved in (13 per cent) was a campaign against a particular Conservative Party policy. People clearly want to 'do' politics on the ground.

We have already laid out the case for more flexible types of associational status that have a greater focus on campaigning – and we have argued for increased local organising capacity to underpin this change. We envisage a crucial function of this increased capacity would be offering members training in advocacy techniques and linking people up with opportunities to be a progressive voice in non-party organisations, such as the many public service governance bodies that are currently open to members of the public. Another key focus would be for local parties to liaise with and draw in local opinion formers as a key part of their activity – particularly in those constituencies without a Labour MP – in order to develop the kind of social networks needed to build long-term political support.

Here, strong lessons could be learnt from the US. Barack Obama's campaign for the Presidential nomination, for example, provides a social networking service (MyBarackObama.com), which not only offers standard networking facilities, but also provides a full set of campaigning tools for individual use: the wherewithal to organise and advertise events, e-fundraising tools, blog hosting services, and so on. Labour is beginning to build on these new possibilities through innovations such as LabourSpace and MpURL's, but still has further to go in developing the tools to allow our grassroots to engage as effectively in outward-facing advocacy as our counterparts in the US.

Cultural changes

Whether by taking political education more seriously, developing new parallel institutions or engaging in community-based advocacy, the requirements of driving fundamental shifts in public opinion will require serious culture changes at all levels of the Party and throughout the broader movement.

In particular, it will require the Government to get serious again about how to use the Party as a site for those aspects of its activity that need to be re-politicised; and it will require the national party to develop expertise and capacity to deliver this, and to take the membership more seriously as a potential campaigning force. It will require local parties to see community campaigning and liaison with opinion-formers as key parts of their activity; and it will require members to engage in outward-facing campaigning. It will also require other progressive campaigning organisations to pull their weight in shaping public opinion, as well as trying to shape government policy.

It will also need the Government and Party to realise they cannot do it all by themselves, to open up, and be prepared to work with others. Most of all, it will require progressive individuals and organisations to feel comfortable with the responsibility for driving opinion change themselves. This would amount to a fundamental rebalancing of the relationship between the Party, the movement and individuals interested in progressive change.

"

5 | Conclusion
A new culture within the Party

Over the last three chapters, we have traced how political and civic life – and the competitive context it implies for the Labour Party – has changed beyond recognition. Changes in citizens' lifestyles and associational behaviour have meant that they now want very different things from political participation than they did a few decades ago – and there are more progressive organisations out there offering it. The erosion of voter loyalties and party identification, meanwhile, has transformed the electoral landscape that parties face, requiring them to campaign for, rather than rely on, votes – though whilst this has brought increased vulnerability, it also offers new opportunities to proactively shape public opinion and build party support among different sections of the electorate.

Our analysis suggests that these trends have two critical implications for how the Party must adapt to remain a competitive force for progressive change in the coming years:

- **Rather than a 'one size fits all' approach to participation, the Party must adopt a more tailored 'variable model', while improving support for existing activists.**
  As Chapter 3 showed, restoring the Party's fortunes as a vibrant participatory organisation will involve a fundamental change in its offer: more opportunities for member activism and a wider set

of other possible associational links, delivered through enhanced and more professional organisational capacity. In particular, we propose a new engagement arm to facilitate the involvement of members and non-members in different types of participation. Crucially, our polling has shown that there are many people who are potentially open to becoming involved with the Labour Party, but do not wish to become members.

- **Labour needs to organise to shift public opinion and build long-term support.**
  Labour should adopt a more strategic view of how to drive the long-term entrenchment of a progressive consensus. This goal should drive a transformation in the organisation and ethos of the Party and broader movement. In Chapter 4, we looked at several ways in which the Labour Party and the progressive movement need to become more geared towards shifting public opinion and building long-term support for Labour. These included developing both the willingness and the strategic capacity to re-politicise its policy narratives and arguments, and developing the right tools, opportunities and networks to disseminate them. We propose the development of outward-facing advocacy networks, through which members, supporters, local parties and other organisations can work in partnership with, though independently of, the Government and national party. In particular, we propose seeding new campaigning organisations in the areas where we will need to frame and win political debates.

A more pluralistic culture

Crucially, we have also seen that these changes in the electoral landscape have required parties to become more centrally managed and professionally led. Though unfashionable, we do not balk atreiterating the point: in order to survive in this new electoral landscape, parties need some key top-down aspects of their operation – though as we also saw in Chapter 3, evidence from leading NGOs suggests that strong central organisation is paradoxically also critical for creating the well-run local participatory organisations needed to engage citizens and bring in new members.

The debate about Labour's organisational structure is too often seen as a zero-sum game focused on the central question of who wields ultimate power over the party; the leadership or the activists. Membership involvement is seen as being at the expense of leadership power, while any aspect of centralisation is seen as necessarily detracting from the activist experience.

Our intention has been to break out of the narrow debate between top-down and bottom-up visions of the Party. Both are monolithic in the sense that they are motivated by the assertion of one policy perspective over another and that aspects of diversity that threaten this are therefore unwelcome, whether it be the strangulation of debate at the top, or the exclusion of wider groups of people from deliberation at the bottom.

The implications of our earlier analysis and the thrust of our proposals are centred on the idea that the key to renewing the party and meeting the most pressing challenges it faces is less to do with changing power relationships in the Party, than creating a more pluralistic culture.

By pluralism, we mean several things. At a local level, a welcoming attitude where different shades of opinion are valued and no-one claims the exclusive right to the 'Labour' perspective, and where we value different levels of contribution, no matter how small. For the leadership, it means being comfortable with a pluralism of voices and opinion in party activity and being prepared to involve and work with others – both members and sister organisations – in promoting the cause. And for the movement as a whole, it means being prepared to see shared interests and objectives across a range of positions, coupled with a sense of responsibility to promote these objectives despite the differences that exist.

Indeed, the Party leadership should recognise that pluralism can be a real benefit if allowed to flourish in the right way. A potential disadvantage of the classic moderniser vision of a rigidly unified party, all 'on message', is that it can tie the Party's identity too closely to specific policy decisions on which there may be real disagreement within the movement and public. On an issue like nuclear power, where it is difficult to relate particular preferences to Labour's underlying philosophy, it is surely to our advantage that the public see there are voices in the Party both for and against? Particularly in instances where ministers are prevented by the constraints of office from giving voice to instincts that many members share, Labour could make far better use of key voices within and around the Party – such as the PLP Chair or the NPF vice-chairs and policy commission chairs – to articulate these instincts and reassure key constituencies.

We need a new ethos within the Party, from elected members to CLP chairs. From the central Party, we need a recognition of the need for more voice for members and acceptance of a more pluralistic culture, including a greater willingness to work in partnership with others in the progressive movement. From members, we need a realistic understanding that the leadership needs flexibility and an acceptance of the involvement of non-members. And from the wider movement, we need an acceptance that it is everyone's responsibility to win the public argument. It will not be easy, but if we can make it work, the new culture and structures proposed here offer a chance for the Labour Party to rise to the very real challenges it faces today.

Epilogue: Why Labour needs a 'Clause V' debate

We believe that the secret of navigating debates about reform lies in turning this from a discussion about how to distribute power within the Party to one about how to give voice in a pluralistic culture and build capacity for advocacy and action. Our polling comparisons of Labour and NGO members described in Chapter 3 cast doubt on the idea that low morale and perceived lack of efficacy is the result of a power deficit. Instead they point to the importance of voice. In particular, this suggests that proposals for improving the Party's policymaking process should focus on improving opportunities for member voice – with more opportunities for input, serious ministerial engagement, and structured feedback mechanisms.

This would also have the advantage of strengthening the way in which members do actually influence government policy: through voice and pressure, rather than through anyone mandating anyone else to do anything (which is simply not how government policymaking works). A key reason why Labour's policy on improving pensions for women and carers is more radical than previously envisaged, for example, was not because of any text agreed or voted upon, but because members had repeatedly raised this issue through the NPF and so ministers had been forced to address it. In this respect, the NPF has been a massive improvement on what went before: it is precisely because its rolling programme and deliberative nature makes it a better vehicle for pressure politics that the NPF affords members much better prospects for influence than a resolutionary system.

Deep down, we all know this is how the Labour Party has always worked in practice, with effective authority over policy resting with the parliamentary party and its leadership, while the extra-parliamentary party exerts a significant (and usually beneficial) influence through pressure politics. Indeed, the Party's Clause V – which covers the party programme – honestly encodes the distinction between NPF policy and government policy (with a meeting of the various parts of the party to agree which parts of the programme will go in the manifesto).

The last vestiges of the myth that members have the power to set current government policy through mandating ministers remains, however, in contemporary and emergency resolutions passed at annual conference. These have now become the place where discontented members and affiliates try to assert their position over the government and cry betrayal when things don't work out like that. Our point is not that debating divisive issues at conference is a bad thing, but rather that the ongoing myth about the status of such resolutions makes the whole process highly demoralising for both participants and observers alike.

When the Labour Party reformed its Clause IV, the process was not only about updating our statement of values, but simply being honest about something which everyone already knew to be the case: that the Party was no longer committed to nationalisation as an end in itself. Similarly, we think an equally frank 'Clause V' debate within the Party is now needed in which we should consider explicitly recognising the status of resolutions passed at conference: that they are important expressions of majority conference opinion on current issues, but that they do not set policy. This could be done in a number of ways, such as formalising the current arrangement, whereby such resolutions are then referred to the NPF's policy commissions for deliberation.

Though it may seem counterintuitive, we believe that more honestly aligning the promise of participation with the reality is key to improving morale in the Party. Not only would it discharge much of the tension and accompanying stage management from what should be enjoyable conference debates, but it could – and should – be one part of a package which looks to reinvigorate the potential of the NPF to better act as a voice for all parts of the Labour Party.

Appendix
Fabian/YouGov topline poll results.
Fieldwork conducted 23-30 April 2007

Section A

Sample A: 1,167 members of leading NGOs. For full details see polling at www.fabians.org.uk

Sample B: 1,209 Labour Party members

Do you agree or disagree with the following statements?	NGO members	Labour members

Table 1

My membership of the organisation has contributed to its ability to achieve its aims	%	%
Agree strongly	18	15
Tend to agree	63	47
Tend to disagree	7	17
Disagree strongly	1	6
Don't know	11	15
Net percentage agreeing (agree strongly/tend to agree – tend to disagree/disagree strongly)	73	39

Do you agree or disagree with the following statements?	NGO members	Labour members

Table 2

The organisation is effective at achieving change on issues that concern me	%	%
Agree strongly	26	17
Tend to agree	64	57
Tend to disagree	5	15
Disagree strongly	0	5
Don't know	5	6
Net percentage agreeing	85	54

Table 3

My contribution is recognised and valued by the organisation and other members	%	%
Agree strongly	19	12
Tend to agree	55	40
Tend to disagree	9	22
Disagree strongly	2	9
Don't know	15	17
Net percentage agreeing	63	21

Table 4

The organisation generally acts in line with my views and beliefs	%	%
Agree strongly	31	13
Tend to agree	61	56
Tend to disagree	2	19
Disagree strongly	1	8
Don't know	5	5
Net percentage agreeing	89	42

Do you agree or disagree with the following statements?	NGO members	Labour members

Table 5

How much power do you feel that you have within the organisation to influence its position on specific issues?	%	%
A lot of power	2	3
Some power	23	25
Not much power	41	42
No power at all	30	25
Not sure	4	6
Net percentage feeling power	-46	-39

Table 6

How much do you think that the organisation listens to the views of members like you when deciding its position on specific issues?	%	%
It listens a great deal	15	7
It listens to some extent	58	47
It does not listen much	10	29
It does not listen at all	2	12
Not sure	15	5
Net percentage feeling the organisation listens	61	13

Section B

Sample: 1,209 Labour Party members

Do you agree or disagree with the following statements?	Labour members

Table 7

Which ONE of these things do you think is most important for the Labour Party to spend its money on?	%
Funding benefits and services to members / supporters	6
Funding membership / supporter involvement in influencing its position on policy issues	15
Funding the campaigning / political activities necessary for it to achieve change on the relevant issues	71
Don't know	8

Table 8

Which, if any, of the following might persuade you to do more? [Please choose up to three things that might persuade you most]	%
If I had more time or the activity was more convenient	37
If I was convinced my extra contribution would make a real difference	33
If I could work on something more relevant to my beliefs and values	21
If I was specifically asked to do more	16
If I could work on something more focussed on the local community	12
If the activity itself was more socially enjoyable	11
If I felt I received more recognition or gratitude for my work	9
If the activity itself was more interesting	8
Other	7
If I felt I received more recognition or gratitude for my work	22

Section C

Sample: 2,591 politically active Labour identifiers who are not party members and never have been. This sample consists of 1,167 Labour-identifying NGO members and 1,424 Labour-identifying people who are civically active in other ways (such as contacting their MP, attending public meetings, etc.). For full details see polling at www.fabians.org.uk

Do you agree or disagree with the following statements?	NGO members

Table 9

Which of these are the reasons why you haven't joined, or become involved with, the Labour Party? [Please tick up to six options]	%
I disagree with the party over particular policies	46
I don't want to do anything more than I'm currently doing	32
I don't have enough time / it wouldn't be convenient	30
I would feel I was giving my support to everything the party does / it would prevent me expressing my values / beliefs	28
I don't think the party would act in line with my beliefs	25
I don't want to pay / can't afford to pay a membership fee	21
My involvement wouldn't achieve anything	19
I don't think it would be particularly interesting	14
I wouldn't be respected or listened to by the party	11
Nobody has asked me	11
I don't think it would be socially enjoyable	10
I don't like politics	8
It's not relevant to the issues that are important to me	6
I don't want to do things as part of a group	5
It's not relevant to my local community / social group	4
My friends / family / work colleagues would think badly of me	2

Facing Out

Do you agree or disagree with the following statements?	NGO members

Table 9 continued

Which of these are the reasons why you haven't joined, or become involved with, the Labour Party? [Please tick up to six options]	%
Political parties can't achieve anything	2
Other	6
Don't know	3

Table 10

If you did get involved with the Labour Party, what type of activities might you most like to do? [Please tick up to three options]	%
Joining a campaign to achieve change on an important issue	39
Working on projects in the local community	30
Monitoring the party's MPs / councillors and holding them to account	25
Taking part in discussions and debates about politics	24
Making my views heard on issues within the party	17
Taking part in the party's policy-making process	13
Social activities	10
Taking part in selecting the party's election candidates	7
Standing as an election candidate / working for the party	4
None of these	14
Not applicable – I shall not get involved with the Labour Party in any circumstances	13

Please say whether you would be willing to do any of the following:	NGO members

Table 11

I would be willing to become a member of the Labour Party, including paying a membership fee	%
Yes, definitely	1
Yes, probably	8
No, probably not	38
No, definitely not	48
Don't know	5

Table 12

I would be willing to become a registered supporter of the Labour Party, not paying a membership fee or having constitutional rights, but receiving things like information and invitations to events	%
Yes, definitely	6
Yes, probably	28
No, probably not	31
No, definitely not	30
Don't know	5

Table 13

I would be willing to support a Labour Party campaign on a specific national / international issue that concerns me	%
Yes, definitely	11
Yes, probably	48
No, probably not	17
No, definitely not	18
Don't know	6

Please say whether you would be willing to do any of the following:	NGO members

Table 14

I would be willing to support a local Labour Party campaign to achieve change within my local community	%
Yes, definitely	13
Yes, probably	51
No, probably not	16
No, definitely not	15
Don't know	5

Table 15

I would be willing to support a Labour Party campaign against a particular Conservative policy	%
Yes, definitely	13
Yes, probably	38
No, probably not	21
No, definitely not	18
Don't know	11

Table 16

I would be willing to attend Labour Party events / debates in my area if they sounded interesting, without joining or registering for anything	%
Yes, definitely	8
Yes, probably	41
No, probably not	23
No, definitely not	21
Don't know	7

References

Chapter 1

1 The Power Inquiry, *Power to the People*, 2006.

2 Power Inquiry, p.29.

3 Society and The Electoral Commission, *An Audit of Political Engagement 4*, 2007.

4 Gallup, *The Gallup International Public Opinion Polls: Great Britain 1937-1975, Volume I*, Random House, 1976. Quoted in J Healey, M Gill, and D McHugh, *MPs and politics in our time*, Hansard Society, 2005.

5 Power Inquiry, p.182.

6 F Mactaggart, G Mulgan, and R Ali, *Parties for the public good*, Young Foundation, 2006.

7 Joseph Rowntree Reform Trust, 'State of the Nation' poll, 2004.

8 British Election Study (www.essex.ac.uk/bes/)

9 *An Audit of Political Engagement 4*, p.30.

10 P Norris, *Democratic Phoenix: Reinventing Political Activism*, Cambridge University Press, 2002.

11 *An Audit of Political Engagement 4*, p.43; *Eurobarometer 66: United Kindom*, 2006, p.22; and C Bromley and J Curtice, 'Where have all the voters gone?', in ed. Park et al, *British Social Attitudes: the 19th Report*, Sage, 2002.

12 MORI, personal communication.

13   *An Audit of Political Engagement 4*, p.41.

14   This discussion draws on D McHugh, 'Wanting to be heard, but not wanting to act?', *Parliamentary Affairs*, 59 (3), p.546-552.

15   *An Audit of Political Engagement 4*, p.50-1.

16   Power Inquiry, p.103-4 and p.230 .

17   M Russell, *Must Politics Disappoint?*, Fabian Society, 2005.

18   P Webb, *Democracy and Political Parties*, Hansard Society, 2007; and T Bale, P Taggart, and P Webb, 'You can't always get what you want: Populism and the Power Inquiry', *The Political Quarterly*, 77, 2006, p.195-216.

19   Power Inquiry, p.145, p. 254, and p.143.

20   P Taggart, *Populism*, Open University Press, 2000.

21   J Hibbing, and E Theiss-Morse, *Stealth Democracy, Americans' Beliefs about how Government Should Work,* Cambridge University Press, 2002.

22   *Power Inquiry*, p.85 and p.106.

23   For lack of consensus on the 'most important issue', see MORI's monthly political monitor.

24   G Stoker, *Why Politics Matters, Making Democracy Work,* Palgrave Macmillan, 2006.

25   *Why Politics Matters.*

26   D Carswell et al, *Direct Democracy: An Agenda for a New Model Party*, 2005. (direct-democracy.co.uk).

27   *Direct Democracy.*

Chapter 2

1   M Russell, *Building New Labour, The Politics of Party Organisation,* Palgrave Macmillan, 2005.

2   J Cruddas and J Harris, *Fit for Purpose, A programme for Labour Party renewal,* Compass, 2006.

3   N Lawson, 'A decade of Blair has left the Labour party on its knees', *The Guardian,* 19 April 2007.

4   P Haezewindt, 'Investing in each other and the community: the role of social capital', in *Social Trends, No. 33,* Office for National Statistics, 2003.

5   M Harrison, 'The British are increasingly stressed, rushed and exhausted', in *Fabian Review,* 2006, vol. 118:1.

6   Citizen Audit, ESRC, as discussed in C Pattie et al (2003) 'Civic Attitudes and Engagement in Modern Britain', *Parliamentary Affairs,* 56, p.616-633.

7   BES data, cited in P Whiteley, and P Seyd, *High-Intensity Participation, The Dynamics of Party Activism in Britain,* University of Michigan Press, Ann Arbor, 2002.

8   The discussion here draws on P Mair, W Muller, and F Plasser, *Political Parties and Electoral Change,* Sage, London, 2004.

9   Mair et al.

10   P Dunleavy and H Ward, 'Exogenous Voter Preferences and Parties with State Power: some Internal Problems of Economic Theories of Party Competition.' *British Journal of Political Science ,* 11: 1981, p.351-380

11   For a recent review of Thatcher's performance here, see R Stubager, 'Preference-shaping: an Empirical Test', *Political Studies,* 51 (2), 2003, p.241–261.

Chapter 3

1   Greenpeace, Friends of the Earth, WWF and RSPB. Figures from P
        Haezewindt, 'Investing In each other and the community: the role
        of social capital", *Social Trends* , 33, 2003.
2   See Table 8 in Appendix.
3   See Table 10 in Appendix.
4   See Table 9 in Appendix.
5   J Cruddas and J Harris, 'Fit for purpose: a programme for Labour
        Party renewal, *Compass,* 2006.
6   See Table 7 in Appendix.

Chapter 4

1   MORI, *The More Things Change: government, the economy and
        public services since the 1970s,* 2003.
2   C Bromley, 'Has Britain become immune to inequality?', in A Park
        et al (eds.) *British Social Attitudes: The 20th Report,* 2003.
3   M Rokeach and S Ball-Rokeach, 'Stability and change in American
        value priorities, 1968-1981', *American Psychologist,* 44, p.775-
        784, 1988.
4   E Carmines, and J Stimson, *Issue Evolution: Race and the
        Transformation of American Politics,* Princeton University Press,
        1989.
5   S Feldman, 'Values, ideology, and the structure of political atti-
        tudes', in D Sears, L Huddy, and R Jervis, *The Oxford Handbook of
        Political Psychology,* Oxford University Press, 2003.
6   See, for example, A Gangl, 'Procedural Justice Theory and
        Evaluations of the Lawmaking Process', *Political behaviour,* 25 (2),
        2003, p.119-149
7   'Think tanks unite in plot to win power', *Times,* 2 February 2007.
8   R Huckfeldt, and J Sprague, *Citizens, Politics, and Social
        Communication,* Cambridge University Press, 1995.

Discussion Guide: Facing Out

The future of political parties and reforming the Labour Party

Facing Out: How party politics must change to build a progressive society by Tim Horton, David Pinto-Duchinsky and Jessica Studdert.

How to use this Discussion Guide

The guide can be used in various ways by Fabian Local Societies, local political party meetings and trade union branches, student societies, NGOs and other groups.

■ You might hold a discussion among local members or invite a guest speaker – for example, an MP, academic or local practioner to lead a group discussion.

■ Four different key themes are suggested. You might choose to spend 15 – 20 minutes on each area, or decide to focus the whole discussion on one of the issues for a more detailed discussion.

A discussion could address some or all of the following questions:

1 Party politics in an anti-political age
Reconnecting democracy is at the centre of political debate. But one common argument sees political parties as part of the problem, not the solution, and that new forms of politics will be more effective in engaging citizens.

- What is the case for the role of political parties?
- How do parties need to change to contribute more effectively to our democracy?

2 Political parties and NGO campaigning
Political parties and progressive NGOs have different roles and purposes, though both seek to bring about political change. The pamphlet examines the attitudes of party members and non-party progressive campaigners towards the organisations they support and their ability to bring about political change, and recommends ways in which parties could change and involve non-party activists.

- What makes people feel that their commitment is making a difference? Where do parties and campaigning groups do well and badly on achieving this? How could they improve?
- How can the Labour Party become a more effective vehicle for campaigners for change? How could it do more to engage individuals and groups involved in non-party campaigning, nationally and locally?

3 Shifting public opinion
A key argument of the pamphlet is that the Labour Party places a high priority on organising election campaigning but not enough emphasis on how to bring about long-term public opinion change.

- How could the party use its policies, and the values under pinning them, and campaigns for further progress to shift public opinion? How could this work in practice?

■ What role could party members, supporters and affiliated groups play in winning public arguments and building support for progressive causes?

4 The future of party reform
The pamphlet argues that Labour will need reform to reverse its membership decline, to become more outward-looking and campaign effectively for change. Is party reform needed, what form should it take, and how can all parts of the party be involved in the debate about reform.

■ Could changing the way that the party makes policy give members more of a voice? How could the roles of party institutions – including local parties, affiliated organisations, the annual conference and the national policy forum – change to achieve this?

■ Could Labour do more to involve non-members, without undermining the role of current members?

■ How should local parties change the way they work and campaign, and how could the central and regional party organisation support and enable this?

■ What would you identify as the most important priorities for future party reform?

Please let us know what you think

Whatever view you take of the issues, we would very much like to hear about your discussion. Please send us a summary of your debate (perhaps 300 words) to debate@fabians.org.uk. We would like to publish comments alongside the discussion guide at www.fabians.org.uk and in the Fabian Review.

Join Britain's only membership-based think tank

Join the Fabian Society and receive a free copy of 'Narrowing the Gap', worth £9.95, **plus** the Fabian Review environment special issue, **plus** the next two Fabian pamphlets. Call 020 7227 4900 or email us at info@fabian-society.org.uk for more information.

Featuring: the rise of
the neoprogs

Fabian Review

www.fabians.org.uk

Summer 2006

THE WORLD AFTER BUSH

In this global issue

Sadiq Khan on being a British Muslim

Jack Straw on increasing Labour Party membership

Andrew Jones on what's been achieved since Live 8

Nick Pearce on Francis Fukuyama's neocons

Hannah Jameson on Joe Klein's *Politics Lost*

PLUS:
Ed Balls in Gaza

Gordon and Hillary

Wishful thinking? Brian Brivati on the special relationship

Interview:
Paddy Ashdown
returns home

Tom Hampson asks about Blair, Bush and whatever happened to 'the Project'?

Nicky Gavron

50 years on from the Clean Air Act, the Deputy Mayor asks if we can tackle climate change like we cleaned up London's smog

The Fabian Essay

"On a bright, cold day in January as the Washington clocks strike twelve, you might just, if you listen carefully, be able to hear a swooshing sigh of relief as it travels around the world. As the 44th President of the United States takes the oath of office at noon on the 20th January 2009, George W Bush's Presidency will enter the history books.."

Read **Sunder Katwala**, p17>>

The quarterly magazine of the Fabian Society   Volume 118 no 2   £4.95

The Fabian Review, Summer 2006

Fabian Review

www.fabians.org.uk   Autumn 2006

BRITAIN AFTER BLAIR

LABOUR CONFERENCE SPECIAL

SO WHAT NEXT?

JOHN DENHAM
CHARLES CLARKE
DEBORAH MATTINSON
SUNDER KATWALA
ANTHONY GIDDENS
LOUISE BAMFIELD

The Fabian Profile
Can Ségolène save France? The
dream of a Royal presidency.

The Fabian Essay
Roy Hattersley on why Labour's next
generation need Crosland.

PLUS: Five things our new prime minister needs to know about women voters

The quarterly magazine of the Fabian Society   Volume 118 no 3   £4.95

The Fabian Review, Autumn 2006

Fabian Review

FABIAN CONFERENCE SPECIAL

www.fabians.org.uk — Winter 2006/07

TEN MORE YEARS

BUT WHAT WOULD HAVE TO CHANGE?

The next decade
Five challenging essays on foreign policy, education, life chances, democracy and the environment.

The Fabian Interview
Balancing Westminster and west Yorkshire. A day with Yvette Cooper in Labour's heartland.

The quarterly magazine of the Fabian Society   Volume 118 no 4   £4.95

The Fabian Review, Winter 2006

THE ENVIRONMENT SPECIAL

Fabian Review

www.fabians.org.uk

Spring 2007

GREENING POLITICS

BUT WHICH VISION WILL DO IT?

PETER HAIN
ELLIOT MORLEY
MICHAEL MEACHER
EMILY THORNBERRY
CHRIS HUHNE
TIM SMIT
JEFF ZITRON

What does red-green really mean? David Miliband sets out his 'next decade' vision of the environment

Progressive or prophet of doom? Matthew Taylor asks Mayer Hillman whether we can live up to him

PLUS: Women's votes will decide the next general election, says Seema Malhotra

The quarterly magazine of the Fabian Society   Volume 119 no 1   £4.95

The Fabian Review, Spring 2007

Special offer: join the Fabians for just £9.95 and get this book free.

'The Fabians ask the most difficult questions, pushing Labour to make a bold, progressive case on taxation and the abolition of child poverty.' — **Polly Toynbee**

FABIAN SOCIETY

Narrowing the Gap
The Fabian Commission on Life Chances and Child Poverty

How can we make poverty history at home?

One in five children still grows up in poverty in Britain. Yet all the political parties now claim to care about 'social justice'. This report sets a litmus test by which Brown, Cameron and Campbell must be judged.

'Narrowing the Gap' is the final report of the Fabian Commission on Life Chances and Child Poverty, chaired by Lord Victor Adebowale. The Fabian Society is the only think tank with members. Join us and help us put poverty and equality at the centre of the political agenda.

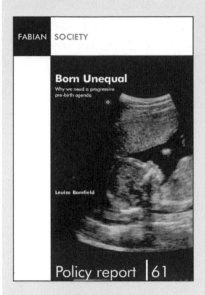

Why we need a progressive pre-birth agenda

In Britain, by the time a baby is born, its chances of living a healthy, fulfilling life are already decided. Building on 'Narrowing the Gap', **Louise Bamfield** examines the reasons for inequalities at birth and explores the ways in which government can act to support maternal and foetal health.

While the Government has begun to recognise the need for a pre-birth policy, it has yet to make a progressive case for it. This policy report argues that the Government's attack on child poverty and inequality risks being undermined by the punitive public narrative that has emerged in recent years around anti-social behaviour and the politics of 'respect'. If action to tackle inequalities before birth is to gain the support necessary carry it forward, the Government must make the case for a progressive pre-birth agenda.

How to break the hospitals' grip on the NHS

In this Fabian pamphlet, **Dr Howard Stoate MP** says that the Government's future NHS vision will fail if they cannot find a compelling public argument which can win locally against the 'save the hospital' brigade.

Challenging the Citadel: Breaking the hospitals' grip on the NHS sees health select committee member Dr Stoate and Bryan Jones argue that the NHS is far too focused on the hospital as an institution.

The new NHS should be about public health and health prevention, and if the dominance of the hospitals continues we will find ourselves unable to make substantial improvements in health outcomes, and the NHS will be ill-equipped to cope with the pressures it will face in the 21st century.

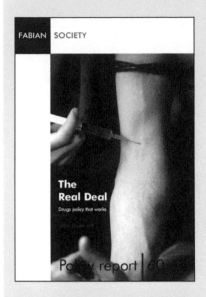

The Real Deal: a drugs policy that works

In the Fabian policy report *The Real Deal: Drugs policy that works* the senior backbencher **John Mann MP** set out the case for a radical overhaul of UK drugs policy.

Mann argues for a new approach to drugs classification, and for compulsory drugs treatment for addicts involved in crime. He says that "coercion should be recognised as not only legitimate but necessary to get users off chronically addictive drugs such as heroin" and says that concerns about civil liberties are misplaced because "free choice" is meaningless for serious addicts.

The report's recommendations seek to address the links between drug addiction and crime, based on work done in John Mann's Bassetlaw constituency where the decision to treat drug use as a medical problem massively reduced drug-related crime.

Labour's Choice: The Deputy Leadership

Hilary Benn, Hazel Blears, Jon Cruddas, Peter Hain, Harriet Harman and Alan Johnson.

In 'Labour's Choice: The Deputy Leadership', the six candidates for the deputy leadership set out why they should take over the post and outline their visions for the next decade of progressive politics in Britain.

As Labour marks an unparalleled ten years in power, the elections give us a chance to weigh up the achievements against the tasks left undone.

This pamphlet, edited by Tom Hampson, gives a unique insight into the thinking going on at the heart of the Labour Party and government.

The 21st century case for Scotland and Britain

There was a time when saying you were British meant you were probably white and probably a Protestant. But today saying you are British should not indicate the colour of your skin, your creed or culture. It must mean that you believe in fairness, in equality and in social justice.

This spring sees the 300th anniversary of the 1707 Act of Union which created the United Kingdom. As the nations and regions of the world seek greater integration but at the same time strive to retain their distinctive identities, the Act of Union is not a historical curiosity, but a blueprint for international co-operation in the 21st century.

In 'Stronger Together', **Gordon Brown** and **Douglas Alexander** set out powerful arguments in support of the Union and explain why the case is strengthened by the challenges we face, not weakened by them.

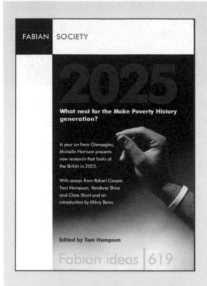

Will the Make Poverty History generation lose its commitment?

Britain came a long way between Live Aid in 1985 and Live 8 in 2005. The Fabian pamphlet *2025: What next for the Make Poverty History generation?*, edited by **Tom Hampson**, asks what the next twenty years could hold.

What positive vision for 2025 is needed to keep the British public mobilised? Despite Live 8, individualism is now stronger than community.

For the first time since 1994, according to our Henley data, a majority of people says that looking after ourselves is more important to quality of life than looking after our communities.

Hilary Benn, Robert Cooper, Tom Hampson, Clare Short and **Vandana Shiva** set out their own visions of global change and the politics needed to make them a reality.

JOIN THE FABIANS TODAY
Join us and receive two Fabian Reviews, plus our
award-winning equality report, 'Narrowing the Gap'

I'd like to become a Fabian for just £9.95

I understand that should at any time during my six-month introductory
membership period I wish to cancel, I will receive a refund and keep all
publications received without obligation. After six months I understand my
membership will revert to the annual rate as published in *Fabian Review*,
currently £31 (ordinary) or £14 (unwaged).

Name	Date of birth

Address

Postcode

Email

Telephone

Instruction to Bank   Originator's ID: 971666

Bank/building society name

DIRECT Debit

Address

Postcode

Acct holder(s)

Acct no.   Sort code

I instruct you to pay direct debits from my account at the request of the
Fabian Society. The instruction is subject to the safeguards of the Direct Debit
Guarantee.

Signature   Date

Return to:
Fabian Society Membership
FREEPOST SW 1570
11 Dartmouth Street
London
SW1H 9BN